THIS BOOK
BELONGS TO:

*For John and Viv Burton, who have spent
a lifetime preserving the pattern   N.D.*

For Mark and Feste   E.S.

WALKER BOOKS
AND SUBSIDIARIES
LONDON · BOSTON · SYDNEY · AUCKLAND

First published 2017 by Walker Books Ltd, 87 Vauxhall Walk, London SE11 5HJ • This edition published 2018 •   4 6 8 10 9 7 5   • Text © 2017 Nicola Davies
Illustrations © 2017 Emily Sutton • The right of Nicola Davies and Emily Sutton to be identified as author and illustrator respectively of this work has been
asserted by them in accordance with the Copyright, Design and Patents Act 1988 • This book has been typeset in Gill Sans MT • Printed in China • All
in Publication Data: a catalogue record for this book is available from the British Library • ISBN 978-1-4063-7889-4 • www.walker.co.uk

LOTS

The Diversity of Life on Earth

NICOLA DAVIES

illustrated by

EMILY SUTTON

How many different **kinds** of living things
are there on our planet?

One,

two,

three,

LOTS!

Yes! There are LOTS and LOTS and LOTS.

From big things like elephants
and oak trees ...

There are two kinds
of elephants, African and Asian,
and more than 600 kinds of oak trees.

to small things like mushrooms ...

So far scientists have counted 100,000 kinds of mushrooms.

and microbes.

Microbes are so small you need a microscope to see them.
There can be 5,000 kinds in just one teaspoon of soil!

Everywhere you look there are living things.

In deserts ...

on islands far out to sea …

FEATHER MITES

under the feathers of birds
and on the backs of beetles ...

Lichen beetles have
tiny plants growing on their backs.
This helps them to stay hidden and keep safe.

*The bright colours in this pool
are made by microbes.*

even in places where you would think
nothing at all could live, like boiling volcanic pools.

Counting how many **kinds** there are can be difficult
because some places are hard to look in …

like the tops of tall trees in the jungle …

or the
bottom of the
coldest seas.

It can also be difficult because, sometimes, things that look different are really the same ...

YOUNG QUEEN ANGELFISH

ADULT QUEEN ANGELFISH

or things that look the same are really different.

VICEROY
BUTTERFLY

MONARCH
BUTTERFLY

But mainly it's difficult because there
are just so many of them!

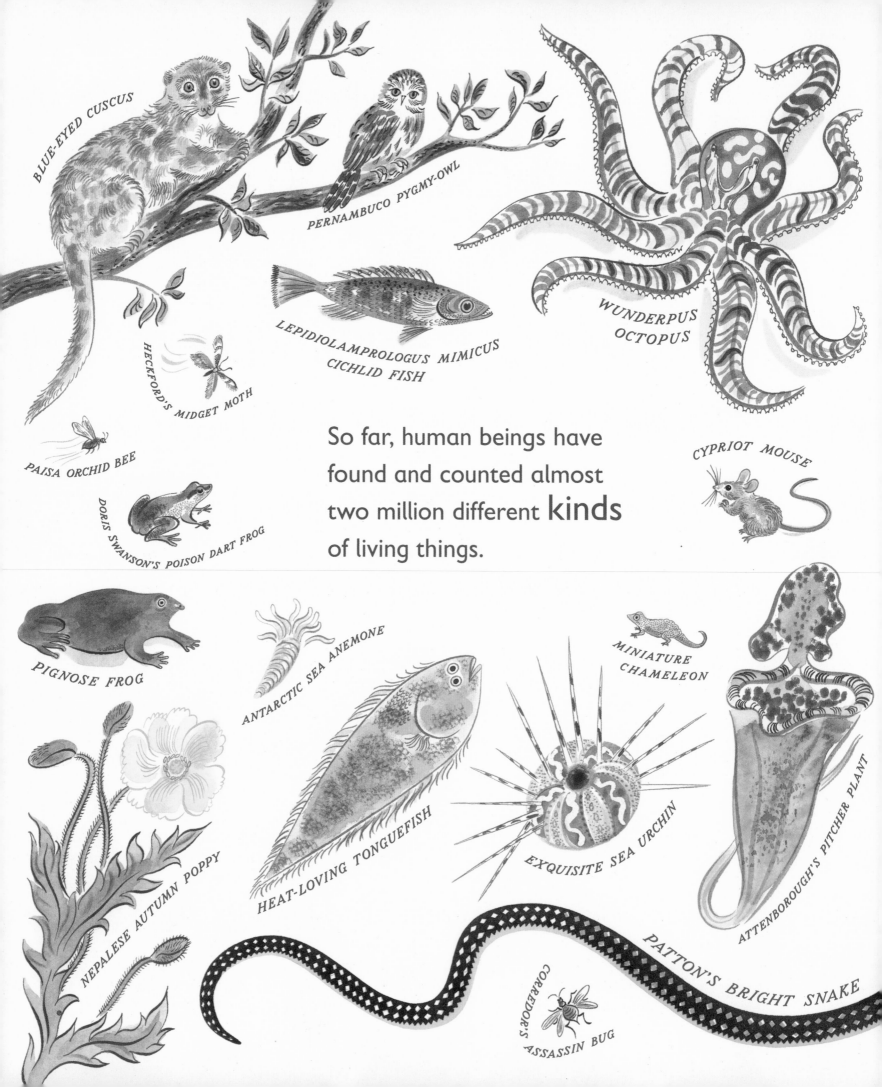

So far, human beings have found and counted almost two million different **kinds** of living things.

BLUE-EYED CUSCUS

PERNAMBUCO PYGMY-OWL

WUNDERPUS OCTOPUS

HECKFORD'S MIDGET MOTH

LEPIDIOLAMPROLOGUS MIMICUS CICHLID FISH

PAISA ORCHID BEE

CYPRIOT MOUSE

DORIS SWANSON'S POISON DART FROG

PIGNOSE FROG

ANTARCTIC SEA ANEMONE

MINIATURE CHAMELEON

NEPALESE AUTUMN POPPY

HEAT-LOVING TONGUEFISH

EXQUISITE SEA URCHIN

ATTENBOROUGH'S PITCHER PLANT

CORREDOR'S ASSASSIN BUG

PATTON'S BRIGHT SNAKE

SWALLOWTAIL APPALACHIAN TIGER

GÁLAPAGOS ROSY IGUANA

DIAMANTINA TARANTULA

ANDRE MENEZ'S CONE SNAIL

SHOCKING PINK DRAGON MILLIPEDE

CRYPTIC FOREST-FALCON

But that's only the start. There could be many millions more. Thousands of new kinds are found every year.

SIAU ISLAND TARSIER

"BARBIE PAGODA" FUNGUS

GREY-FACED SENGI

"SPONGEBOB" FUNGUS

CHILD OF CYPRIS TINY FISH

BONAIRE BANDED BOX JELLY

GOLDEN V KELP

All the creatures on this page have been found in the last 50 years.

TENNESSEE BOTTLEBRUSH CRAYFISH

And the more we find, the more we learn about how living things depend on each other – for food, for places to live and for ways to grow.

Jaguars eat pacas which eat the fruits and seeds from trees.

Hummingbirds eat insects and nectar, and insects eat nectar.

Toucans live in tree holes.

Bats bite holes in leaves so they droop to make a tent.

Pacas poo the tree seeds they've eaten, which grow into new trees.

Baby frogs grow in pools of rainwater in leaves.

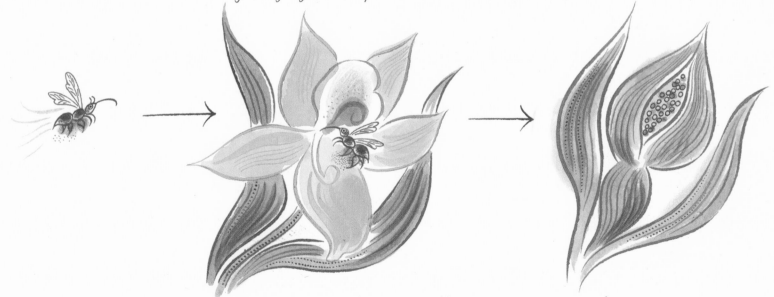

Bees carry pollen to flowers so flowers can grow seeds.

We have learned that every
kind of living thing is a part of a big,
beautiful, complicated pattern.

The trouble is, all over the world, human beings
are destroying bits of the pattern ...

POISONING THE AIR, RIVERS AND OCEANS

TAKING TOO MUCH FROM THE SEA

BUILDING ROADS THAT CUT FORESTS INTO PIECES

so that animals
and plants disappear.

EXTINCT

MAUKE STARLING

MADEIRAN LARGE WHITE

CAROLINA PARAKEET

ZANZIBAR LEOPARD

PYRENEAN IBEX

RÉUNION GIANT TORTOISE

DODO

TASMANIAN WOLF

Many kinds of living things have already been lost.

SPECIES

DELCOURT'S GIANT GECKO

BUSH WREN

MASCARENE PARROT

NORFOLK KAKA

PASSENGER PIGEON

GOLDEN TOAD

LAUGHING OWL

MAURITIUS BLUE PIGEON

MARTINIQUE CURLY-TAILED LIZARD

CHOISEUL PIGEON

EASTERN HARE-WALLABY

GOULD'S MOUSE

VIETNAMESE JAVAN RHINOCEROS

Perhaps some have disappeared, even before we've found them.

Human beings are part of
the pattern too, and we need to
make sure it stays big, beautiful
and complicated ...

because we could
not live on an Earth
where we had counted
down instead of up ...

from LOTS

to one.

Also by Nicola Davies and Emily Sutton:

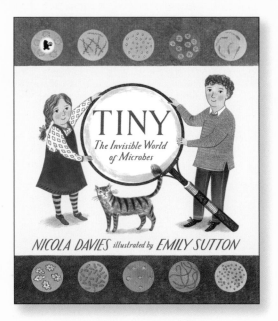

ISBN 978-1-4063-6070-7

There are living things so tiny that millions could fit on a dot.

Although they're invisible, they are everywhere. And they're busy doing all sorts

of things – from giving you a cold and making yoghurt to wearing down mountains

and helping to make the air we breathe.

Find out in this amazing book how the smallest things on

the planet do some of the biggest jobs.

"reveals the miraculous-ness of science with sheer sharp-edge precision and decorative charm"

Sunday Times

WINNER OF THE SLA INFORMATION BOOK AWARD

Available from all good booksellers

www.walker.co.uk